Beautifully $\mathcal{B}$

Beautifully Broken

McKenzie Rockweiler

Charleston, SC
www.PalmettoPublishing.com

Beautifully Broken
Copyright © 2022 by McKenzie Rockweiler

First Edition

Paperback ISBN: 979-8-8229-0122-3
eBook ISBN: 979-8-8229-0123-0

Preface

This book is about what it felt like for me to be torn apart; it doesn't exactly mean that being broken is beautiful. Being abused by someone and going through trauma doesn't make you beautiful. What makes you beautiful is what you become after having to go through that. I do not recommend staying in a situation that you know is bad for you just for character development. Everyone becomes who they are differently, but that certainly is not the way.

I created these poems out of hope that maybe someone will find their own light.

Contents

PART THREE: THE TRANSFORMATION....... 71

Part One:

Inner Child of Mine

Therapist friend

The one everyone tells everything to,

the one who can never catch a break,

when they need help, it is somehow too much for everyone else,

and they are simply too busy.

The person who feels guilty talking about their own life,

feels weird when people notice that they aren't okay.

The person who smiles even when they are dying inside.

This is the person who breaks down when they are alone.

The silent crier.

The overwhelmed, forgotten—until it is too late—friend.

ADHD

Is when you can't stop thinking, but then can't completely remember what about

When you wonder the what if's of the world

Your mouth running faster than you can form words

The wish to fly free from a trapped world

The need to move to focus

When prescriptions are the answer to an empty void

Being the class clown, overtalkative, then too shy

Never enough, but always too much

Time doesn't exist, yet it holds me back, and I am accountable

I feel very vulnerable with all the information that I spill

Numb zombie in another land and completely dreaming about another planet

Energetic child, annoying teen, chatty

September 7, 2015

∼

Some of My Questions, the Answers

Where will I go? Anywhere we want to, Love.

Where does this path go? To a new destination!

When will it end? No one knows, so let's enjoy every second.

Who can I trust? Yourself, always trust you, my love.

Who should I trust? You will know when you meet them if you should.

What kind of world do I live in? A beautifully broken one.

How much will I change? You have changed so much in the best of ways.

Will I even change? Of course, we all do, Love.

Did I make a wrong turn somewhere? No, if you did we wouldn't be where we are today.

Am I in love? Yes.

Why is life confusing? It isn't always, and being confused can be a sign.

Where are the answers to my every question? Right here, Love.

Am I good at what I do? You're good at the things you're passionate about.

Does he really love me? It was love, but not true love.

Will it be a forever love? No, but you will always remember.

$\sim$

Why are people insane? They have lost their way and themselves.

Am I insane or just crazy? Neither, just a little lost, but I got you.

Should I be afraid? No, but when you are, know I am here.

Are my tracks right? Of course, Love, your path is your path.

How is the future? Difficult, but it leads to a better place—I promise.

What will I do with my life? That is up to us, Love.

How is seventh grade? Seventh grade was challenging.

Scared of My Own Shadow

I went from feeling free

To being on chains again

I went from no care in the world

To being lost in the dark

I went from flying, to falling

Why does the world work this way?

Makes you feel unstoppable then puts you through hell.

The universe asking me when I will finally learn my lesson

Hellfire surrounds my inner light, making it burn to hold onto

Trying to find myself, so I search for a lighthouse

I am a boat, and the waves are getting bigger; the storm is wicked

I feel as though I am sinking

All I see is the fog

Little did I know I was right by the light

All I had to do was venture

My Heart

My heart needs care

My heart needs love

My heart is fragile

My heart is breakable

Why play with it?

Take all it has

What bad has it done?

Why is my heart broken?

All it has done is give you all it had

My heart deserves love

My heart deserves late-night conversations

I deserve to feel safe

To be open

To run wild and free

My heart keeps beating

It took time to heal what I didn't break

But I took each and every step

Learning the things I know now

~

What I deserve

What I dream

What I can have

Are simply all the same things

Keys

You have the key to life

You have the key to a heart

You have the key of knowledge

The key of creativity

The key of being evil

The key to listen

You have these keys

Love

Bravery

Confidence

Friendship

Those are the keys you earn

Every key unlocks a new adventure

A path, a story

That story is yours

All of these keys unlock new chapters in your life

Which key will you choose first?

Which key is next?

~

This Monster

The monster inside has taken control of me.

What am I becoming? What am I doing?

The monster inside, just beneath my veins.

Filled with rage, jealousy, sadness

Prepare for a nightmare

My monster is in control

This is the monster inside me

Filled with anger

Filled with "I shouldn't have to be better"

Wondering why years of my life seemed to be easily tailed off

Trying to breathe in and out, but fire comes out

Raging teenager they say was all to blame

What about the bruises on my skin when I was just a kid?

Now let that sink in

I was a kid, but no one cared, so why should I?

This monster inside

Is truly just misunderstood

Someone unloved

～

Put off

We have different priorities

But it was never me

Grew up too fast

In a world so broken I couldn't see

That the person trying to save me was me

Mom?

A mother

Cares for you

Helps you along the way

Holds your hand

Gives you a shoulder to cry on

Helps you

Loves you

Gives you advice

Tries to help you understand life

A mother, a friend is

Nurturing

Compassionate

Honest

Someone I dream to be someday

I promise to forever love you

To teach you

To guide you

And to help you

I will mess up

I will not be perfect

But I will be accepting

I will be a good mom

The Broken One

The broken one came crashing down

To a bleeding fall, a broken angle

Lost faith, trust, the will to fly

A broken one is no longer free

No longer willing to try to get up

A broken human has scars

Has gotten lost in the maze of life

Has gotten hurt too many times

A broken one who was hurt

May be healed only by oneself

Lost all things that mattered

And wonders if such thing will happen again

Undercover Bitch

Acts sweet, kind, helpful

But waits to break you when no one can see

Tries to get in your head

Two faced

Tries to make you fall

Has a goal to get you on their level

The level below the sea, below hell, complete darkness

They want you to feel pain, ruin your life

Someone you know until they take their mask off

The oil to your water

The poison to the air you breathe in

∼

My Past

So far, yet so close

I don't want you to know

Sometimes I have no choice but to tell you parts

Piece by piece you will understand

My heart has stitches, but it must go on, now beating fearlessly

Gotta keep living

No longer hiding the broken parts of me

Gotta keep going

Sometimes I get lost in my mind

Rewinding time without a time machine

Simply all with a trigger

My darkness is a part of me

Self-acceptance is the key

One Second

I'm mad; I'm screaming

I'm careless and falling In love

Crying like it is raining

Screaming away the pain

I could be glad

Lost in the world confused

Having fear in my eyes

No longer recognizing myself beyond these emotions

When Will I Learn?

To stop giving chances

To stop trusting easily

To think before I do

To listen

To tell the truth from a lie

To be free

To stand up

To not be afraid

Crying

The words you say hurt

Knowing I am a part of you

The things you do hurt me

The things you say hurt the worst

Every time you scream, my heart throbs

It hurts knowing I might be like you

Emotional bullets forever engraved in my brain

Words repeating like clockwork

Young child held to high standards

Never enough

Failed

Gets hit with emotional destruction

Left with emotional scars

Known for being overly sensitive

Who Will I Be?

Will I be like my mom?

Will I be like my dad?

Have to work all my life.

Will I be me?

I don't even know who I am.

Who am I?

What will I choose?

Will I have control over myself?

Will I lose myself?

Abuse

Kills you on the inside

Kills your mind and burns your soul

Can you heal from it? The cure is healing

Hard to heal when you're stuck in darkness

When you see shadows and have scars

Takes on multiple forms

Sometimes is naked to the human eye until symptoms arise

Makes you feel trapped inside your own mind

Losing trust within yourself from someone else's words

Listening to voices that aren't even yours

Doing things out of fear

People pleasing to survive

Creating a burning fire on the inside with a self-destruct button

Sometimes it hits you so bad that it gets hard to function

Emotional Abuse

Something you can't stop a person from doing without leaving entirely

The words attack you on the inside

Destroying your heart and everything you have left

Sudden darkness and complete blindness to your surroundings

Crying yourself to sleep at night questioning every breath you take

Vision blurs, breathing slows, mind empty

Lurking

As I walk into the shadows

I wonder who I am

As I walk through life

I see it for what it is

As I observe the world

Questions are made

As I lurk in the shadows

I start to find who I am on the inside

As I observe life

I realize what it can be

As I see the world

I still wonder about the possibilities

~

The Unknown

As I walk in the twisted, dark path

I realize there are so many words unspoken

So many things unheard, unnoticed, unseen

When I enter the ally, I gaze up at the stars, thinking about what we are becoming

Lost

Forget what we have done

All I see is darkness

Forget about the dreams we had

All I want is the truth

Forget everything you know about me

All I see are lies

Forget the words that were said

All I want is a hand to hold

Forget my appearance

All I see is a reckless world

Forget about me

All I want is a way out

Forget who I was

All I see is what we are becoming

Forget what you were told

All I see is something that wasn't written in stone

Forget what I have seen

All I want is for people to see what I see

~

Long Sleeves

Fake smile

No one sees the pain

She holds on strong, hoping everything will be okay

She hides what was given to her

She hides the cuts, scars, and bruise

She hides the pain with her smile

Hiding the pain she can't explain

If her demons were no longer there, would anyone care?

She hides the tears that have been there for many years.

Hide what I wrote, hide what I felt

I hide the truth

My Shadow

My shadow, my only friend

The thing I live for is my shadow

My current home

My inner child

My trauma

My thoughts, emotions

Roller coasters of commotion

Never felt the peace of the ocean

Layers of pain

Breaking Old Habits

Old habits transition slowly fading,

Voices still corrupt my vision and ability to speak

Being assertive

Or being too much

I can never tell what is what in these moments

Of a dark haze where voices blend

And suddenly words come out of my mouth in a blaze of fire

I slowly work through these habits

I find my voice

I find myself

Slowly separating the voices

Regaining my vision

Difficulties

High emotions, stronger destruction

All it takes is one little trigger

One blast, one bad moment, and I feel absolutely fucked

Drowning

Weighted down by the anchor that clings to my chest

Attached to the anxiety of not knowing what happens next

But I'm trying my best

Breathing in for ten seconds

One, am I enough?

Two, shut the fuck up

Three, where's my good luck?

Four, it will be okay

Five, life comes and goes in phases

Six, you're so strong

Seven, think of the sun hitting your face on a warm, breezy day

Eight, what colors do I see?

Nine, I still have this problem to face

Ten, I still have memories that can't seem to be erased

Habits developed early on becoming patterns

But now seem historic

No longer relevant

The voices are still heard

Problems relevant but solutions follow

~

Letting go of everything that isn't me

Which wolf do you feed?

The one that has glowing eyes

That tears everything apart in its path, creating a bloodbath

Or the wolf that protects, brave, strong, the one that howls at the moon, and runs free in between the trees.

Tiny Soldier

Someone who had to grow up fast

Facing the world young, feeling blinded by the reality of it all

Childhood missed

Parks weren't seen

People were unknown

Blinded

Thinking this is how life goes

~

As I Wait for You

As I wait for you, I don't feel at home

I feel the fear coming back to my eyes

Waiting for a better day to come along

I wonder what you're doing

If I am a waste of your time

All day, all night

The fears I once fought come back

Stronger

I fear I won't make it far

Me, Myself, and I

I am not weak but strong.

Throughout my whole life, all I have been trying to do is hold on.

I am not who you wanted me to be, but therefore I may never be.

I am not normal but different, but then again who isn't?

I am not full of hope, but that doesn't stop me from dreaming.

I will not lead, but I do not follow.

Just because I'm quiet doesn't mean I don't have anything to say.

I'm finding myself more every day while I am picking up the broken pieces you left me with.

I don't change, yet I don't stay the same.

Depression

Feeling hidden, no one sees you

Even on your bright days, you're still dark

The darkest of nights is when the clouds roll in

Down comes the rain

Happy but still sad

Shape-shifting who I am

Mixed emotions, brand-new potions

∿

The World

This world is full of darkness

Broken things, broken people

Full of monsters

Two-faced people

Others scared to be who they are

A misleading society

Misunderstood teenagers

Words feel like gunshots in the mind

We face life with uncertainty

Darkness can teach you

But someday maybe that isn't all we will see

Depression Feels Like

The feeling of being lost, being scared, complete emptiness.

Feeling like there isn't anything left for you.

Being broken, needing something to fill that empty space.

Hopelessness in this life, believing giving up is the right answer.

You feel the life drained out of you, giving up on the things and people that mean the most to you.

Realizing there is nothing but darkness surrounding you and this empty feeling.

Pushing others away so you don't feel guilty for numbing the pain.

If there is no one there, then there is no need to explain.

Thinking of every fear, every regret, keeping me weighted onto my bed.

Every mistake feels like it had just happened, can't help but let the guilt creep in.

Becoming lost in the world and no longer knowing yourself.

Worried that you can't be found, because what is there to be found?

~

Hero

Healed my scars

Stitched my heart

Gave me my light

Found my key

Helped me see the world

Helped me grow

Taught me to fly

Made me realize who I am

Made me realize who I want to be

My hero gives me

Love

Life

Friendships

And they will forever be my hero

I'm Human

I make mistakes

I have problems

I am not perfect

The question is who is?

Yes, I have regrets

I can be unmotivated

I can be different

I change

I have emotions

Words hurt me

Actions can break me

But I fight for what I believe

I feel pain

I can fake a smile

I can be happy

I can fall down, but I promise I will stand right back up

~

Older

Time is slipping

I'm getting older

Can't get younger

Every second that passes is another second into the future, which is currently the present

Too young to understand

But too traumatized to not know

I know what I didn't know then

Time is limited

Every second counts

Every move you make matters in the future

So I can't regret what I haven't done, stop whatever I am doing, and do what makes me smile

Otherwise it's all a waste

≈

Love

Beautiful like a rose

Powerful like the moon

Different each time

Waiting for it to bloom

Waiting for the right time

Feelings change

Making mistakes

Track

Am I on the right track

On the right train?

I got forever to go

Completely guessing the way

What door is open?

I have scars from the past

Questions about the future

What I hold within me is the present

I put myself on the right train

I'm doing the right things

To become the person I know I can be

∾

The Breaking

My thoughts are thinning into the air that surrounds me

Turning into fog before fully existing

My mind is a puzzle with missing pieces

The deeper I go, the more I fall

No parachute

Everything left behind

Mirror image of others still not enough

Lost myself trying to save everyone else

Searching for light, but I'm slowly caving into the madness

Understanding nothing

Looking at myself with confusion

Feeling unbelievable heavy

Trying to break this fake illusion

No one listening

Can't hear a thing

Don't know if I want to be saved

Had to be brave

Put up a shield, made indestructible walls

～

For my own protection

But it was never enough

Part Two:

THE
LETTERS
OF
LETTING
GO

Intoxicated

I loved the old you, the person you used to be. Somehow you went from being Batman to being the Joker. What we had became this toxic bomb.

I felt trapped in that chair where you put your hand up and down my thigh, even though I said, "Stop, no, stop."

I opened my windows for you to see, gave you everything I had left. I was a Little Red Riding Hood. You were the Big Bad Wolf, but instead of eating my grandmother, you made me feel at home. But before I knew it, that house came with a lock and key. You left me inside that place we called home and set it on fire. You always came back to put out the fire.

There was so much smoke that I thought you were my firefighter when really you were the fire starter. I felt locked up in this thing we called love, when love isn't what we had at all. At first it was a flicker in the flame, but then the candle fell and started a forest fire that we were dancing inside of. You were the Joker, and I was your Harley Quinn. I was so caught up in the love I had for you that I didn't see who was holding the gun, who was pulling the trigger, who was lighting the matches. My windows shattered as the crackling of the fire roared. I was so obsessed that I was the issue, I thought I was the fire starter for so long. Then came a day that you were caught for cheating, cheating on me with so many others. Soon staying up until dawn, wondering if I was the problem, thinking if I looked better or if I was different became my normal.

Still your hand goes for my thigh every time. Still you try to touch my skin. And when you do, my body becomes an earthquake. I am suddenly stuck to the chair, the ground. The air becomes harder to breathe, even when I say no, you still reach. This was the moment I realized you were the one behind the gun, the one pulling the trigger. You were starting the fires that burned me alive, only leaving me to pick up the pieces. You would only come back when I was done, when you wanted something, because that's what I am. I am your hot cocoa on a rainy day. I am the game you don't know how to quit playing. Now I am wearing flame-repellent clothes; I can see clearly through the smoky haze. I took the bullets out of the gun you used on me. I can finally breathe again; this is a game that is out of commission.

I see the game you played on me for years crystal clear now; the red lights flashing in my face are no longer ignored. If you touch my skin, it still turns cold. I still feel as if I have become frozen over, but this ice has been broken. I am no longer stuck here, frozen.

Dear Anxiety

You tear me apart every day, every night.

Suddenly it turns into a seed that has been planted inside my head

It grows stronger unknowingly, which makes it harder to unroot when fully grown

I start to crumble to the ground

Not this time, anxiety

I will not ask that question

I know the answer

I will not let you wonder any further just to leave my body restless in the present

I'm a good person

You tend to remind me how at one point I wasn't

I am a good, sweet, loyal, kind person

I worry way too much, and you give me a whole list of reasons why

While I burn down that list before it's even finished

The best part is I know I am worth it

I am more than worth it

So what you got, Anxiety?

~

I have armor, meditation, breathing techniques, and art

Anxiety, you suck the life out of me most days

You bring me back to bed and ask me how life is worth living.

I have so much to live for, so much to see and do.

So I only have one thing to say to you, Anxiety, after billions of things you have said to me.

Fuck you, Anxiety

Sleep Habits

Sleepless nights fighting with myself

Overthinking the past

Wandering to a different place not far from here

From not sleeping at all

To sleeping consistently

Personal bad habit

Two naps a week for me, if not too careful can turn into an everyday habit

No energy left inside of me until I can't do anything but shut my eyes

A hard thing to break

My mind goes just five minutes, which leads to three hours

Not wanting to leave the comfort of my bed

From "It's okay to nap," to "Where have you been?"

Not noticing the weeks go by

Because it was only just a nap

Which leads to late nights sitting up by myself

Watching TV and starting other bad habits

At this point it's self-isolation

No motivation

Meeting my greatest defeat

I'm either up all night

Or up early in the morning and don't fall asleep until twelve

At least with one habit, I see the sun

Get things done

Eat three meals

And live life

With other one

I find depression to be my latest obsession

Self-isolation to be my greatest weapon against myself

Dear Person Who I Thought Gave Me Love

Slowly I lost parts of myself I didn't know I could lose

Became a person I didn't know I could be.

I lost my ability to say no and gained the ability to please.

An endless fight between my boundaries and your anxiety.

I was convinced that I was a problem. My shorts were too short, my thoughts were too loud, I was too bold.

I remember having the need for comfort but giving you every second of my attention.

Every night I questioned my reality, losing all sense of gravity.

I always spoke too much, never did enough, constantly in the wrong.

I lost every part of myself trying to fix every part of you.

Giving you second chances like they were tickets to a carnival.

There's a song you showed me that somehow became my favorite but now it just sucks all the oxygen out of me when I hear it.

Looking back it feels like a movie, where you yell at the person on the screen, telling them to run away.

It was not your fault but mine, right?

The emotional roller coaster of our trauma bond will forever be engraved in my brain.

Dear PTSD

You follow me in my dreams, flooding me with memories

Waking up struggling to breathe, it's weighing down on me

Certain smells bring back certain visions, reminding me of what type of reality I used to live in

A feeling that drops me to the floor, not wanting to feel this way anymore

Thinking I can escape with the pills that I take

Temporary fix not trying to hold on to this

Hellfire burning in my stomach as a response

I wish I could press pause, let this resolve in my mind

But I don't have that kind of time

Comes back like clockwork

Sending chills down my spine

Body aching all the time

Falling from a fifty-story building, waiting for the crash

Thinking it was all karma

Inner child healing is refacing all the locked doors, burnt down memories, rewriting everything that's left of me

Changing shirts after awakening, hoping no one will notice that I woke up sweating

≈

Face feeling like fire from something I don't want to remember

But I have constant reminders

'Tis not something I will run from

But I wonder what will come from this

Sometimes I wish my PTSD was just a bad dream

Like everyone said

Until the doctor said PTSD

It's like a silent secret about where it came from

Can't talk about the past that haunts me

To you it doesn't exist

For me it's my daily dose

I dealt with my trauma

It still haunts me from time to time

PTSD is forever

So I come with a few warning labels

Don't scream, don't touch, don't get violent

I will fight or flight

I have more rage than I can cage

I have years' worth of tears

It made you stronger

Funny I didn't need to be

For I was a child. I needed a childhood, not to be misunderstood.

~

Dear Panic Attacks

Am I dying, or am I gonna live another day?

Is what I ask you every time you spread hellfire throughout my body as a trauma response. My heartbeat racing faster than a race car, wondering how many more laps of this I can take before my engine shuts off.

A million unfinished thoughts and possibilities swarming my hazy brain.

Falling asleep to sound—without it the demons are here, the air is thick with fear.

Overthinking my actions to people's words and their reactions to mine.

Emotional Tidal Wave

A riptide current

Crash and burn

My own thoughts causing this disaster

Falling into a deep depression

Down a rabbit hole

Losing my way

Facing the battles every day

Tired but can't fall asleep

Flashbacks of all these memories

Questioning what I see

Unexplainable physical pain

From my damage

Feeling unfixable to shattered

Confused by everything

Happiness caused by the little things, shortly fear follows

I never knew that freedom could feel so hollow

Denial

Couldn't leave the vines you wrapped around my mind, just in case they turned into a beautiful garden.

A push-and-pull lever.

Running just for you to follow.

Admitting I felt trapped was a hard pill to swallow.

Confused by your mixtape of our conversations.

Walking into a battlefield

Stepping around the bombs

Masking the feelings I felt inside

Isolation is what kept me here

Waiting for this feeling to disappear

Self-esteem being ripped in front of me

Words burning into my soul

Losing one's sense of self

Unmotivated, survival instincts activated

Defending your actions to the end of me

Self-blaming eating up your table turning of words

Drowning in hope of change

Rearranging my mind

～

Puzzle after puzzle never solved only disorganized

A house but no home

Cracked foundation that no new location could fix

Not daring to take my time that was no longer mine

Stripped of my identity

Left not knowing what is left of me

Seeing a different reflection

Endless apologies, same behavior

Repeating patterns

Love Bombs

Love trip of a fake fairy tale

Pink pixie dust sprinkling hope

Fake sense of safety, false sense of reality

Real to me but a game to you

Acting like a Sour Patch Kid on repeat

First you're sour

Got all that toxic masculine power

Then you're sweet

Treating me like a queen

Take away the green screen

Shape-shifting my reality

Broken promises

Future faking

Playing dollhouse

Drowning in fake love

Falling before the step was even taken

~

Two Years

Threw my past in my face as if I was to blame

Cold sweat

Burning nausea

Long nights, constant fights

Drowning in your words as they crash down on me

Feels like I'm hit in a tidal wave waiting to be saved

Scared of wrong choices

None were ever right

Doubting myself every moment

Avoiding your eggshells, around them was broken glass

Imagine that

Thinking I was to blame for everything

Your mind manipulation drove me insane

My mind became another game for you to play

Two years wasted, slowly I faded

Learning what the opposite of love means

There was either yelling or silence

Both meant the same thing

～

I ask for things based off my clothes

Showing things they were exposed

Feeling ashamed for the clothes and how they shaped my body

Feeling unheard

Constantly being compared to someone who didn't like me

Asking why I couldn't be her

My insecurities rising, knowing I could never compare

I would watch you stare; I don't think you ever cared

Drowning

Drowning in the thoughts in my head

Losing my every breath

Flashbacks are mini heart attacks

Dissociation losing myself mid conversation

Still questioning my past reactions to how you were acting

Still lost and confused inside my own mind

Trying to figure out how I wasted so much time

Can't seem to focus

Still under that hypnosis

Can't seem to cope

Feeling this weight on my chest

All this anger inside

Feels like I'm going in a circle

One minute I'm fine

Then everything crosses my mind

All this negativity that I need to release

But somehow you still get to me

Survival mode gotta rewrite this new code

Dear Old Me

Sad, confused, abused

Hurt and breaking inside

Filled with confusion

Not knowing what's right or what's wrong

Lost in a mirror maze

But every reflection you see is different

Not knowing what's real

Run, oh, I wish you ran

I know we aren't runners

But this wasn't your monster

It was someone else's, and they were tearing apart your soul

Take every part of you to fill up their broken pieces

Always feeling like something was missing but never knowing what it was

The word "no" forgotten

My words I choked on

My mind was something I couldn't count on

That's when you go

It wasn't safe

I saved us, but I wish I could have told you

Letting Go

I'm letting go of the memories

Of everything you said to me

Everything you have done

My mistakes

My words

The illusion for what you could have been but never were

Of the things I thought were real

I am letting you go

I am letting us go

Like seeds in the wind moving to whatever is next

Energy being sent back to where it once came

Hope restored in all its glory

Stepping off this roller coaster that was our story

I wish you the best for whatever happens next

~

Forgiveness

Healing myself because of somebody else, but

Forgiving them

For not knowing how much construction it would take for me to rebuild my foundation

That broke from their destruction

Forgiving them

For feeling so much pain inside that they had to share that broken feeling

Forgiving them

For shattering me like broken glass

Forgiving them

For bringing fog to my mountains and tears to my eyes as if it needed to rain

Forgiving them for carrying on a cycle, for they cannot see the light of day

Forgiving them

But mostly forgiving me

I forgive myself

For staying not knowing if you'd change

For drowning in hope

~

Looking for an antidote

I forgive myself

For losing every part of me trying to save every part of you

For I am no handyman

I forgive myself

I forgive you

CPTSD

Multiple forms of trauma

Never-ending memories

Always healing

Always breaking down

My nightmare leaves me waking up in flames of hell

Emotions taking on a physical form, causing an ocean tide of pain

Ready for the next roller coaster

Confused by the peace I feel

But enjoying it

The seeds of anxiety eating away inside of me

New insecurities from past experiences

Fucked up midday mind trips

Uncontrolled dissociation

Waking up in new locations

Times changing without notice

Never-ending loop on full blast from the past

Feeling as if I'm going to crash

Looking for the flip switch

Just switching to different traumas

Not knowing which one to heal first

Constant when, where, who, why

Inner critic is my latest alibi

~

Part Three:
The Transformation

Self-Forgiveness

I forgive myself for not accepting help

For my past mistakes

For who I was

For losing myself

For thinking I could save everyone else but not trying to save myself

For talking bad about who I am

For being the world's doormat

I am worth love

I am worth someone's time

I am worth it

I am worth the time and effort I put into myself

I am my first priority

I am so beautiful

I am uniquely smart

I am determined

I am more stubborn to solve that riddle

~

In the end it is me

In the end I am happy with myself

In the end I give my all

In the end I do what I know

In the end I learn from my mistakes

In the end I am full of love, light, and acceptance

Transformation

A butterfly in a cocoon

Changing with the phases of the moon

Inner reflection

Loving oneself

Acceptance of my flaws

Growing wings

Evolving minds

Rising above

No longer blending in but standing out

A new beginning to an end

A rainbow after a thunderstorm

Change

I am my own first priority

Self-focused

Becoming my hero

Saving myself

Putting in the time to heal my mind

Going through the maze not getting stuck in this place

Figuring out the life I want, putting the pieces together

Releasing who I am not

Becoming who I am

Being honest

Being real

Setting my boundaries

Putting my needs first

Loving myself the way I deserve

Falling only to jump right back up

Some days are harder than others, but I always push through

~

Eventually clouds clear

Even if it has to rain a little for the sun to finally shine

~

Healing

Feeling my emotions moving with the waves

Letting this anger fade away

Unlearning what I learned

In the cocoon

Painful emotions stir in like fire

Accepting the pain I carry

Acknowledging the past

Connecting the dots from the beginning

Learning from my mistakes

Letting it all go

Finding inner peace

Accepting who I was then and who I am now

Loving who I am becoming

Being mindful of how the flowers grow

They push through the seed growing in the dark slowly

Once they reach the light, they still aren't done

~

I have reached the sun

Being kind to myself

Taking my time

Letting these feelings show

Letting myself grow through the pain

Pushing through the hard days

Thriving either way

Taking it day by day

Realization

Younger me would look up to who I am now

Inspired by my wisdom

In awe by my beauty

Bad bitch energy, that is what is meant for me

In this moment my highest potential I have not yet reached

But I reached the highest part for younger me

Giving her balance, stability, and love

I am the person she wanted me to become

Now the picture shifted

I know my highest peak is yet to be reached

But I made it through many dark times

Have finally reached my time

On my way to better days

Self-accepting

Resurrection

Proud of who I am

~

Recognizing the person I see

Loving the way I see things

Understanding the capability I have

~

Self-acceptance

Hard to find

Deeply looking toward myself

Find the differences between who I am and who I once was

Loving both

Loving my flaws

Loving who I am becoming

Accepting who I used to be

Accepting my past mistakes

Taking in the experience

Learning to love every moment

Turning I'm Sorry into Thank You

I'm sorry for talking so much

Thank you for listening

I'm sorry that I have to work though my trauma

Thank you for loving me even though I have healing to do

I'm sorry about breakfast

Thank you for appreciating it

I'm sorry for being clingy

Thank you for holding me a little longer

I'm sorry I gotta do this really quick

Thank you for reminding me about free will

I'm sorry I am going to accomplish my goals

Thank you for your support

I'm sorry it took me so long to respond

Thank you for being patient

I'm sorry that I'm still unlearning survival tactics

Thank you for potentially waiting

Thank you for calling me beautiful

Thank you for supporting me even on my hard days

Thank you for asking if I am okay

Thank you for being sweet

Thank you for making me breakfast

Thank you for treating me with respect

I found my independence

I found my slice of inner peace

I have found forgiveness

I found myself

Balance

Peacefully searching for happiness

Never wanting anything less

Unloading the burdens in my mind

Making the time right, you know I'm gonna be kind

Taking the weight off my chest

Piece by piece putting that shit to rest

Finding my peace

Before I become deceased

Shifting realities, there goes my gravity

Waking up from the complex mind games

No longer feeling shame

Reprogramming my mind

Time to be kind

Mental health, taking care of oneself

Trying to find peace in the hell

See it in my eyes; I know you can tell

Going through the guilt

Feeling everything I felt

Letting it all go away

This is my day

I'm off to a better place

Feeling full of grace, finally in my place

Financial stability invested in me

Relationship, time for you and time for me

Is exactly what I see

Doing what I need

I'm planting all the seeds

Yin and yang

Breaking all the chains

I'm finally free

It's time to be me

Believe

Better thoughts

Better choices

Better solutions to my own personal evolution

Small changes making all the difference

The right amount of water and sun

The flower blooms

It blossoms

It opens its beauty to the world

Eventually weathering away

Completing a cycle

Of transformation in rebirth

Self-acceptance of one's past mistakes to no longer feel burden

Accepting one's flaws, the old wounds that left scars, the bags under one's eyes, my face and how it's not clear all the time

Accepting where I was and where I am

Knowing within where I could be

No longer feeling like a victim, but I'm a warrior

~

I went through different stages of hell

But took the flame and became a dragon

You can see it in my eyes

See it in my walk

Hear the way I talk

The heat, how it comes right off my tongue

∼

Inner Critic

Why do you make me feel like the world that's on fire is my doing?

You tell me that the changes in the faces around me are my fault

No one will accept the happy dances in the starry night

The random hobbies that I find extreme passion for

You say no one can handle the brokenness I feel inside

No one could possibly accept me through all my healing stages

You laugh at me every time I look into the mirror showing me all the broken parts of me

All I see are my flaws

Thank you for pointing out the parts of me that needed that extra love

My scars are my tiger stripes

My body is a canvas filled with a story that has evolved

I see a person who tries their hardest

Who has climbed the hardest mountain, then had to do it all again

But looked down and appreciated how far they have come

The world falling apart is not my doing

∼

I can rebuild my own home, make one plant into a forest or a garden

Who doesn't love a girl who dances beneath the stars, in the rain on a beautiful summer evening?

I love thriving and being driven from my independence

If a person cannot handle who I love to be

Then they simply aren't just meant to be

I am more than enough, and I am nowhere near being too much

If I am too much, too happy, too depressed, too adventurous

Then they aren't on my ride anyway

They don't roll with the tide

They don't dance by the fire with every burning passionate bone in their body

They simply aren't in my lane

You can't force someone to switch lanes

Everyone has their own car

Some cars need more work

Some cars come brand new and don't need any upkeep

I guess I am an old-fashioned, wild car that does have upkeep

But I am a beautiful mint-colored 1957 Chevrolet Bel Air

~

I need to keep working hard on myself, so I can keep moving forward

Nothing had come easily to me in this life, and I wouldn't expect it to

But I have found enough fire in my soul to thrive in this adventure

I have found enough love in myself to keep up with this engine of mine

I have found enough motivation to take a look at my breaks and change my oil

I have found enough passion to keep up my paint job and take care of my old-fashioned, beautiful seats

I have found enough love within me to no longer need it from anyone else

Thank you for your concerns, Critic; however, they have been worked through and now passed

Comfort Zone

Comfortzone is only knowing what you know and following it even if it is a trap

Outside of comfortzone could be absolute freedom but is always adventure

A leap of faith within yourself

A step everyone has to take at some point, willingly or not

Not everyone was born into a safe place

Some people's safe places are houses on fire

They rely on the fire, the heat coming off someone's breath, the constant yelling, the heightened emotion, constant commotion

Others know safety, find comfort in their needs and expectations being met

While others keep begging for the bare minimum

The ones that have been born into dragons learn how to maintain the flame

They step out of their comfortzone to heal and deal with their emotions

At first peace feels like a soaring fire blazing all around them, their thoughts echoing, creating their own chaos

And chaos feels like peace because it is a pattern, and they know what to expect

After the chaos has been dealt with, in their peace they find happiness within themselves

They find happiness within the world and within people

But the dragon knows how fast this happiness can disappear

They know all the negative emotions and for the first time feeling euphoric, experiencing the positive ones

Almost like a new drug their mind just can't wrap around

The people born into safety not knowing the dangers the world holds

The people made into dragons only seeing warning signs and trying to heal, not overreact to how they feel, making sure that what they are experiencing is real

We tend to feel like good things only last so long, so we look for things that aren't there

Our minds become the fire we either have to dance with or we add oil

We step out of our comfortzone to set our wings free

We take flight

We take the fire we were given and ignite it, turning it into strength

~

Finding Me

Expected immediately to know what I am good at

Not even knowing who I am, only what I have been through

Just broke through the storm

Comparing myself to everyone else

Different timelines, different stories, different outcomes

Finding my hobbies

Finding the passionate fire inside of me

Understanding what I deserve

Not forgetting what I know

Changing my habits

Recentering myself

Racing thoughts, brainstorming

Everything I like raining down on me

A voice inside me screaming, "Which one do I pick?"

The world is ending

There is only so much I can do now

~

Do I heal?

Do I change the world?

Do I make art?

Do I have enough time?

Taking the time for myself

Finding my career but letting it change with each part of my story

Changing as a person pulling away the curtain

Taking this time to shine

Explosive Creativity

I see the world as broken

People misspoken

Everyone searching for that winning token

Something can be rebuilt

So I must paint on every broken city

Bring the light to the dark

Create a lighthouse for each place or storm

Start something for people who need to find freedom when no help is there

Create a beautiful safe space for kids who come from a fiery place

Making anything that comes to mind

Going with the flow of the pencil as words fall from my mind and onto the paper

Painting my emotions with each stroke

Visualizing the different colors from each thing and how they make me feel

Taking pictures of the places I love and how we left them

~

Click as the picture forms

Hopefully it's beautiful, it's clean, it's a start of a new world

Dancing to the beat even if I look silly

Building my confidence from scratch like it's the best bread in the world

Making sure I have all my ingredients and take my time

Creating what I wish the world was into what it could be

Hopefully you can see it before it's too late to

Recreate, rebuild, know where we stand and how we got here

Acknowledge our past, but do better in the future, create better in the present

Patience

Paper thin

Found waiting

Created on how we feel in silence

Waiting for something we wanted

Steps being taken

Pages being turned

Good things coming

Stillness

Waves crashing slowly against the sand

Volts of electricity shifting in the mind

Change of thoughts

Running through the forest

No longer escaping my mind but embracing it, clearing the fire

Planting the seeds of a new future

Inner Child

Crying all alone, not knowing where to go

Needing to be held, to feel safe

Missing out on so many things

Trying to help people communicate

Being seen as grown up from such a young age

So tired you could sleep for days

Fighting to survive but feeling like the walls are caving in

Like you did so wrong by simply existing

Truth is

Your childhood was stripped away from its innocence

You weren't taught how to love

You weren't taught to trust

People look at you and say "tragic"

You were a mistake

You made mistakes

You didn't know how to react to how you felt

~

You didn't know what you were feeling

Let alone how to express the amount of emotions, so hyperaware of everyone around you, just so you know who to look out for, so you don't get hurt again

But you are a happy little accident

But you now know how to express how you feel

My love, I will protect us

I will never let us go into harm's way

We can dance

We can laugh as loud as we want

We can say what we feel

We can blow bubbles while the sun hits our face

We can walk into the woods, listening to the sound of the leaves blowing in the wind, the birds chirping, and deer running through.

We can watch the sunrise and the sunset

We can hide under our blanket and read a book

Inner Teen

Burning hot coals beneath your feet

Fire coming out of her mouth as she speaks

A girl who was in so much pain

Constant flashbacks of a childhood she didn't get

Screaming things that she couldn't forget

Things were ignored, problems from the past buried very deep

Always told she needs to watch how she speaks

Never safe, couldn't trust, founded so much lust

Scared of love that she didn't know

Scared of people getting way too close

Pushed everything away

Tried to hide everything she felt inside

Then this anger turned into a dragon of some kind

She could no longer deal with the family blame

The burdens on her back

All the scars on her legs

The early abuse

Mad that no one saved her

Felt like no one could hear what she had to say, it didn't matter; it was way too late.

Kept hearing "only a few more years"

As the anger built up, a fire soared inside

Burnt down every lie she could no longer hide

The tears built up behind a dam came flooding down, she broke down those one-hundred-year-old walls

Felt abandoned, felt unseen, thought she could be replaced

Stuck in a toxic cycle not knowing why

Lost sight of who she was

Saw the damage that was done

You can say what you need to say

You can do what you need to do

Be who you need to be

You do not need to carry the burden, the abuse, the lies, the guilt

It isn't yours to carry; it is yours to let go

You protected everyone but yourself

Then you defended us

Now we have boundaries, when crossed that dragon will come out; she will let you know you crossed the line—you do it one more time, you are gone.

We protect our energy

We love ourselves

However, we need to let go of the fiery feeling against our skin

Feel the grass and flowers beneath our feet, the sun shining on our face, and the fire within us

I love our rainbow flames

So powerful, so assertive, so bold, so protective, and fierce. I love us

Close Diagnoses

I was almost diagnosed to something similar to you

It freaked me out

Because I don't want to be who you are

Then it hit me like a bus

If I can be this sweet, this much of a kind, caring person

You could have been too

You had the choice to heal; you had the choice to treat me better

But you didn't

That is on you, and your mental issues are not an excuse

If I was distracted for five seconds and hit someone with a car

That's on me, not the person

I was distracted, and it was my car

All it takes is five seconds

All it takes is small amounts of effort to change

All it took was putting the work into action

But you were never satisfied with who I was

And that's not on me

I am amazing, I am smart, beautiful, even gifted

You took a look at me and thought you could break me

Little did you know I have walked through the flames of hell

Heard demons screaming in the night

Constantly had to hold my breath

But I healed; I looked at myself and said, "No more"

I am not a door mat, I am not a doll, and I am not a punching bag for your emotions

If I had what you had, that is let alone proof that you had the choice to be better

Then I remembered everyone goes through their own shit

Their own type of fire

Own type of shame

But you put your blame on me

You made your mistakes my fault

And I said I would fix it; I cannot put you back together while you break me

～

For you are not mine to fix

We can't fix others; we can't fix what we even broke

We can heal ourselves; we can show others the way, but that's all

To Think

To think I was to blame

The missing chemicals in your head

That you didn't need help, didn't want it, didn't accept it

It was all me, always me, never you

I have met others with the same imbalance

Not everyone is the same; no one has the same reactions

However, if they can heal, if I can heal, so could you

I cannot blame myself for you not steering your own wheel

For I cannot steer yours; otherwise, we would both crash

For you have a need for speed, and I have the need to relax and fly

You make quick turns, and I make them nice and easy

You press on the breaks just as hard as you press on the gas

I let gravity take the car; I have my foot pressed on the breaks gently coming to a stop

You don't stop at all; you keep going, running off your emotions like they're the ammunition

To your fuel. You speed at their intensity. I pull over and think, I watch life and admire its beauty, breathing in and out before I get back in my car. As you keep going and never look back. I was scared that I was like that; at one point I was. But we are not the same.

We don't have the same story.

You took your pain and made it into addiction and impulses

I was angry, destroyed everything in my path, burned a whole forest down with the words falling out of my mouth before I could even think. Then I saw the smoke, saw me looking back at myself and realized I no longer recognized the person I saw staring back at me.

So I woke up from the nightmare

Woke up from the chaos, the toxicity

I woke up and saw me for who I was becoming and stopped dead in my tracks

A new path cleared

It was the forest I burned down, but there was a new stream

I went to the forest, and I planted seeds, watering them every day

Healing my broken mind

Within time I formed healthy habits

Within time I formed a true smile

Within time I remembered life didn't have to be the warmth of a fire but the warmth of love

Love within oneself, acceptance, love within others.

I realized I could heal

I'm healing my past; I'm healing my inner child who's crying in the corner

I'm healing my teenager who wanted to catch a break and was full of anger and hate

I'm healing me

I am becoming the person I know I am inside

I am recognizing intrusive thoughts; I am using assertive language

And you could too

That was and is your choice; it is never too late to start healing

I forgive you, but I will not forget, nor will I ever come back

I wish you well

Love

I want you to know how I feel

How real it is

But how high I feel when I am next to you

This emotion makes my brain feel euphoric

Like everything we do we are doing for the first time

A double rainbow on a rainy day

The leaves when they change colors in autumn

The first snowfall that falls ever so beautifully on the branches of the trees

I feel worth something

Not just because of you

But the love I have found within myself as well

It's as if I have been given powers that no one can take away

Something I feel in my veins

Knowing my worth when I hear other thoughts

That first step you take out the door

Depending on the weather how your body reacts

~

Confused

Being treated differently

But I like it

I love being loved

Being given more than the bare minimum

Being given trust

Something so real

Everything simply is better by you

Adding fruit to waffles

When it's warm and it rains

When you have a fire and you make food over the campfire

Everything is ever so simply better

The sun shines brighter

The little things are more visible now

Rainbow Flames

Different colors, different emotions

Passionate about what I feel

Red is the anger that becomes a smoky haze

Orange is creative bliss

Blue is intense pillow tears

Purple better treat me like a damn queen

I dig those frequencies

Only match up with people's vibrance

You want to say some stupid shit

You will hear me roar

Be careful when you say something

I'm a fierce one

I got the fiery flame

Those icy eyes

A personality that can't be contained

She's protective

Mad respective

Completely dedicated

Not a worker, but a leader

Voice

Finding my voice

Is unscrambling the words in my mind

Sorting through my own emotions all the time

Being completely real with how I feel

Realizing I have been people pleasing my whole life

Not knowing what I have to say

Confused each and every day

Finding the melody to my beat

Turning my emotions into lyrics

Not knowing how else to feel it

All efforts, all issues aside

Listening to every stop sign

Proceeding with caution

Taking out the noise in my mind

Finding my own words, that's a hard thing to find

I can finally make up my own mind

Who am I?

My opinions no longer tangled into others' thoughts or needs

Becoming my own person again

Unlocking the door I once locked many times before

Taking myself out of the cage I was put in

Saying what I say without my thoughts getting in the way

Filtering the nonsense

Liquid truth coming out of my mouth

Every moment

Is another moment I get stronger

Maybe I'm bold, assertive, happy, sad

Not always doing what I'm told

Pulling away the curtains, never completely certain

That is life, full of mistakes

Constantly pushing, asking if you got what it takes

~

Self-Love

We've come so far

Climbed mountains

Went on emotional roller coasters

Fought the demons from our past

We tackled our insecurities

We worked hard on the things we want to be good at

Our skin glows in the moonlight and is bathed from the sun

Our hair is flowing effortlessly through the wind

Our style is unique and beautiful

Accepting what once was

Accepting the unknown

Loving every scar, stretch mark, imperfection

A canvas full with a story to tell

Another chapter presenting itself

A new beginning

A new me

The me that has always been inside of me

Assertive, strong, bold, creative, intelligent me

I know what I want

I know what I deserve

I know who I once was

I know who I can be

I love every part of me

Me from then and me in the now

I have learned a lot from every mistake

I have formed my emotions into paint strokes on a canvas

How I feel into words on paper

My reaction into a melody

I create magic from my very existence

A beauty so strong it comes from within

Now shines bright on the outside as well

Daydream

Different realities created in my brain a getaway escape

Visions from my past that tend to haunt me

Dissociation finding myself in a new location

Never being completely aware

Spacing out in time

Envisioned

Speaking to different parts of myself

Traveling to different dimensions

Being here, yet in another place

Head filled with clouds

Feels like I'm dancing in the rain on a sunny day

Manifesting my reality

Bringing it to me like I am gravity, but I have wings that help me fly

Feels like I am reaching the sky

I am a star that once exploded

Collected myself

Reborn

And now shining brighter

Maybe I am different

Filled with added chemicals from explosion

Brightly shining

Newly found

Renamed

Renewed

Assertive

How I feel, my opinion, the situation

Never knowing

If I am saying the right thing the right way

Mind fuck, memories unlocked, can't rewind that clock

Being open about my emotions

Knowing what to say

Being me with no regrets

Letters that were once scrambled now form words

No longer falling into a bottomless pit of anxiety

Letting go of everything negative inside of me

Working out even when I'm tired

Resting even when my mind is restless

Letting myself feel

Being honest with myself and others

Showing what I know

Surrounding myself with the right people

~

Communicating with the right people

Not spilling my feelings

But being open about them

Nothing is black and white

Not everything is clear

But I know parts of me

I know what I see

I know what I feel

I know how real this is

To feel something so close that it reaches your fingertips

To say something you feel, but it's turned around

Questioning everything you do

Realizing you aren't a problem

Seeing issues for what they are

Letting thoughts be known but pass

Opening your own book and showing others

~

Make me

Diamonds are created under pressure

Broken things can become something even better

Fixing things with liquid gold

Healing myself becoming someone else

Dancing with the beat

Singing off-key

It doesn't matter what makes me me

As long as I am happy

A rare crystal found in the mountains

A seed that is growing just beneath the dirt

Something so beautiful you can't look away

I am one with the moon going through life with phases

Healing phases

I turned all the pages to meet the people I've met

Starting new chapters over and over again

Denim is long lasting

A leader

A lone wolf in search of a pack

Phases

Things around us change

We evolve into different versions of ourselves

The things we once felt pass

We stop repeating a vicious cycle

We start our own

Growing

Healing

Truth

So much left to do in an unknown time frame

So why not start today?

Freckles appear

Our bodies don't stay the same

It's our mindset that hopefully one day changes

Transitioning from one part of our journey into another

Going with the moment, seeing what it unfolds

~

The Feeling of Love

Love that is real blossoms

It is a wildflower overlooked by many

A dandelion can be used to heal; I wonder if this feeling can do the same

Love is honest, kind, assertive,

It's not all knowing, there are twists and turns; it is an adventure, a climb

But I am here for the journey

It's bittersweet like lemonade

Something I'm no longer afraid of feeling, love is intense

The euphoric feeling when the roller coaster gets to the top, slowly stopping so you can see the bottom, then it moves. Just for a second you've simply forgotten the worries of tomorrow

It is all or nothing

The effort put into deep conversations on a starry night

The little things that bring joy to one another

The moments of bliss where it's movie-like and the world can see that we, too, can be at peace

The moment where you can see a future in someone's eyes

∽

Where your heartbeat changes to match their rhythm

Independently growing but constantly falling into your arms

The fresh smell of flowers

First bite of the food you have been patiently waiting for

It's a process

There are boundaries, there are conversations

Can be what ifs, can be hopelessness

But it is worth it

When you find the one who makes it feel like the sun is surrounding you with warmth

When you don't have to question where you feel safe, where you feel yourself

When you smile so much your face hurts

When you know they are a call away on the rainiest of days

That is the one who will make you cinnamon hot cocoa

That is the one who will remind you of your worth

This is the one who will forever change the way you see love, how it makes you feel

Endless bliss from every kiss

The tingle in your chest when you hear their name

Feeling lighter than a feather, that's the one, that's love

~

Boundaries

A line between what I will and won't allow

Protecting myself

The right to feel

The right to say no

My rights unfolded

Not bad nowhere near wrong

It's a fine line no one should cross

Invisible force field

Do not be mad when you cross said line

When the bombs have been unleashed

It came with warning signs

Crossing it equals a friendship forgotten

A reminder of what I need and want within myself

Minor Setback to Major Comeback

I will not let what I went through break me and turn me into something I'm not

I'm taking a step back, looking at the bigger picture

Who I am, how I'm healing, my journey thus far

Coming back stronger, braver, smarter, and hotter

My intelligence improving

I now have the courage of a lion, hear me roar

The things I can do with my strength are unbelievable

My appearance is feisty

I had to take a step back to take a leap forward

I know now what I did not know then

Healing my trauma from within my DNA

Waiting for the stillness of the water

The wind moving between the trees

Moving with life

Going through the healing phases slowly

Making the needed changes to my mind

～

Changing the future generations and their stories

Protecting the future by being mindful in the present

~

I Am Worth It

I'm worth loving endlessly

I'm worth the effort and time

I'm worth the little things, surprises that make my heart melt

I can breathe in oxygen

I'm drinking water

I look in the mirror saying, "Damn, how'd you get here?"

Not in the way where your body cringes with a tear strolling down your face

I say it knowing I look beautiful tonight

I say it feeling that I can do whatever I put my mind to

I say it knowing how far I've made it

I know I deserve more than the bare minimum

No longer shall I beg for less than

I shall receive what I deserve

Recovering from the bumps in the road

Noticing the light and how it shines on me

～

Shining brightly

Saying I fucking made it

I learned

I took each and every step

Within divine timing I will get to where I'm going.

Temple

My body is my temple

Somehow these walls have fallen

In some way for a long time, my body wasn't mine

It was overtaken and used

I picked up the pieces

I look in the mirror

I see the body that was touched in ways I didn't want

I see something that I can't get out of

I can burn clothes

I can change outfits

But I can't shed this skin of mine that was forcefully taken

I can't shed the feeling that what was once mine seemed to be forgotten

I can't shed the feeling you gave me every time you crossed the line and I shut down

A switch appeared in my mind for the safety of your crimes

Now, finally, I have reclaimed my body

~

My body—what it wears, what it does, everything

It's my body

These are my light-blue eyes

These are my thick thighs that have scars and freckles

This is my beautiful face with freckles by my eyes and a cute button nose

This is mine

I can wear the clothes I feel comfortable in

I can eat what I want

I have the power to say no

I have the power to reinforce these boundaries

I have learned to love this body

Something I used to feel trapped in is something I now feel free in

Long Car Rides

Chasing the sunset, changing my mindset over time

From one destination to another

Head in the clouds, trying to remember

Thoughts spinning fast

Hearts on the floor

Don't know what we are doing it for

It's all work and sleep

Questioning what I eat

Pressing the gas to the floor

All we want is more

Give me a destination

Creating satisfaction within our lives

Driving in the night, looking at the stars

Just finding out who we are

Dancing to the rhythm of our own beat

Gratitude

Noticing how far we have come

Appreciation for what we have

Starting every day with an open mind

Thankful for the little things and how they lead to big things

Becoming more aware of when we smile

Where we feel loved

Surrounding ourselves with the energy we like

Being mindful of life

Noticing the smells, tastes, energies, how things feel

Taking what we receive into consideration

Loving the life we build for ourselves

And recreating our lives when we don't

Our answers only change when we move

As we evolve our lives start to glisten

Slowly the things around us change

The way we look at a sunset

The way we feel around our loved ones

How we look at ourselves in the mirror

~

Restless Mind

Thoughts seem to appear as my body is unable to sit still

Forgetting what I need

Forgetting how soft the soap becomes when it forms bubbles that surround my skin in a bath filled with warm water on a lonely night

Forgetting the much-needed hour meditation to remind myself to breathe, to take life day by day

How good it feels to write on paper with a fresh gel pen that sparkles in the light

The smile that's created once I recognize myself

Freshly putting oil on my lips, making them feel ever so soft

I forgot the happiness I hold within

Little things being forgotten until it stings

Doing things for oneself

Not caring who is listening

Overthinking the thoughts that I already thought I was over

Restless the body, restless the mind

Voices caving in but they are not mine

~

I put on my war paint

Remembering who I am and where I stand

The power within me holds a light

It shines brighter than the sun; be careful—it will blind you

My heat comes in waves

Mindful

Pink cotton candy clouds in the sky

Are my thoughts; I take notice of them as they pass by

Feeling the breeze against my skin

Closing my eyes and smelling the sweetness of the flowers as they're blooming

Noticing how I feel after a run

My heart beating louder

My thoughts silent, not still

Journaling my thoughts

Closely noticing the patterns

Breaking through every bad habit within me

Loving my every curve

Loving my inner child

Relaxing my inner teen, letting her live wild and free

Becoming a happier me

Inner Garden

Planting seeds and watering things you don't see grow right away

Wondering if the effort you put in is worth it

Not knowing if the roots are growing or if the effort is worth it

Hoping

Waiting

Then a tiny little plant rises from the dirt

A feeling of relief fills your chest

Knowing the work put into it has not been lost time

The plant still needs encouragement

Needs the water

The observation

You still need to attend to its needs for it to grow strong and healthy

Forgetfulness of a plant is forgetfulness of oneself

Do you notice the growth and wait to see the results?

~

This Time

I can regret not starting yesterday

I can regret not starting a year ago

Not knowing then what I know now

Or I can keep going

Keep climbing this mountain

Learning and growing along the way

Moving this boulder out of my own way

I can regret the things I didn't get down yesterday

Or I can see today with new, fresh eyes

Get done what I can, what I need to

Be gentle and kind to myself

Be sweet to others

Feeling blissful every day

Not stressing about the little things

Admiring life before my eyes

Following the butterflies

Climbing trees to see the sun as it sets

Waking up in the morning, listening to the birds as they sing

Looking at the staircase behind me, acknowledging how far I have come

Looking at the step in front of me

Going up one at a time

Life is not a race, so I shall take it at my own pace

Travel and see the things I want to see

Jump off the bridge with rope tied to my feet

Float up in a hot-air balloon, being one with the skies

Admiring the feeling I get after I work out

Noticing my confidence growing

My self-love overflowing

Loving the people around me properly

Putting myself first yet having empathy

Knowing I can do it now

Pushing through my own rain clouds

Letting the sun break through

~

Becoming present instead of resentful

Catching Myself

Switching my actions, switching my feelings

Doing all of the healing

Switching my thoughts

Reminding myself I'm safe now

Taking my walls down

Finding myself fumbled in words

Making connections that I never understood

Catching myself loving myself

Catching myself recognizing the person I see

Admiring my own progress

Looking at a bad bitch

Being sweet, loving, supportive

Taking my own feelings into consideration to situations

Knowing my own boundaries

Burning down the necessary bridges

I am my biggest fan

~

Catching myself when I fall, knowing I can get right back up

Feeling in the present, not what's little left of it

Feeling happiness when I see the little things I have dreamed

How my garden has grown

The green trees surrounding me

How reading my book makes me feel supported

Switching my thoughts

Recognizing a safe place

Finding peace in peace

Switching my anxiety, asking just how much of a possibility it could be

Reminding myself of my worth

I'm worth every penny

Making mistakes but learning from them

Give it my all, knowing I will be okay if I fall

~

Carry On

Pushing through every emotion

Pushing through every bad habit created to save myself at one point

Keeping the morning rush

Working out till I can't breathe

Making breakfast big enough that I have to eat

Walking through the dandelions

Learning about who I am and what the world can be

Taking weight off my shoulders, it is no longer mine to carry

Healing the things I didn't break

Finding trust within myself

Finding out about all I have

Traveling through memory lane, pointing to the source of my own pointless navigations

Recreating my route

Sometimes stepping back

In order to leap forward

Step by step

Movement by movement

Changing the little things, creating something better within myself

Raining diamonds around my pink glow

Recognizing my voice and the difference between theirs

Seeing the light even in the dark

Noticing how brightly the stars burn

The sky lit by their beautiful energy

Once they explode

They're gathered and become reborn

Maybe we can do the same

Learn from our mistake, our pain, regroup

Become a new us

A new you

A new me

A new future from a brand-new perspective

Sacred Destiny

Evolve, change, grow

Everyone's sacred destiny is to become the person they want to be

Find love within

Starting to trust yourself

Following your own adventure

Leading yourself

Living to the fullest in your own way

Creating the life you want

Feel at peace and being free

No longer feeling like you're searching for that missing piece

Reconstructing yourself with gold

Knowing your worth

Your personality unique to you

Not a mirror image of someone else

It is to relearn all that we thought we knew

Keeping an open mind

~

Leaving things better than we found them

Spreading forgiveness but not forgetting

Learning from your past and others

Creating something new in the now

Being aligned with ourselves

Accepting change within ourselves and around us

Expanding our knowledge on our passions

Following our hearts

Living for what counts and making it count

Climbing our hills, getting through bluffs

Finding yourself at the top of a mountain, still having so far to go but admiring how far we have come

Different journeys

Different outcomes

Different knowledge

Growing Phases, Moon Phases

Sometimes it's all dark

Other days I am lighter than a feather

Healing what I thought I couldn't

Finding new things to heal, adding them to your personal file

Growing into the person you imagined yet the person no one else knows

Exhausted from the change in transition

Growing up chaotic, seeing everything as normal, not knowing respect

Later on expecting it

Climbing the ladder, taking the leap, not for anyone else but for you

Making your love eternal

Creating conversation instead of chaotic arguments

Fighting the voices in your head that have been pushed into you

Creating a different version of you

Becoming a new you

~

We aren't all born like this; yes, my brain is chemical, but it's also traumatized and reorganized

Creating a tool box of self-care for your body and mentality

Finding what best fits you, not the people you see on the screen

Realizing everyone's list is different

Filling the void with love, reminders of your worth, and the things you love doing, healing it step by step

Just like the moon

When full you have completed that healing stage—that habit is broken, a new one started

Half is when you've completed it, finalized it, but recognized something new you need to heal

Crescent is you figuring out your pattern

New moon is a new thing to heal, new goals, new habits to break, and the new ones you need to create

Then it starts again; you start stopping the bad

As the moon gets fuller, the more of that habit you break and the more you catch on to the new one you're trying to create— you feel more full

More yourself no longer like you are somebody else

~

I see you hurting; you are not a burden—you are full of love and light

Look at the stars at night; sometimes we have a raging fire

But that can be beautiful

For that is what lights up our sky—balls of fire a million miles away

In awe I stare at their beauty

As you should stare at your inner flame and how it changes with you

Reflection

I look into the mirror and notice my beauty

From my curves to my bright-blue eyes; even my scars have a story to tell

I see the person I am becoming, loving the person I once was

Reminding them they were more than enough and trying their hardest

I see the me now loving who I am now

I slip up

I fall

I definitely break

I catch myself and start again

I get back up to finish the race even if I am slow

I take time for myself and heal

I look into my thoughts, seeing much more positive than negative now

∼

Voyage

Taking a journey on the inside only to be seen on the outside

Giving a new perspective on your own life

The journey counts just as much as the destination does

Healing through insecurities is rough

It is emotional and looks different on paper

Everyone has a different script to read and ritual to follow

It is all a process

We have to look around and enjoy the view

Not just let each day pass us by

Instead fill ourselves up with love

Admire the world around us

Take a risk even if it's a leap of hope

Climb that damn staircase because someone has to

Going somewhere fair to find yourself

Deep into the woods or maybe even deep into the city

Trying new foods, clothes, ideas

~

Taking that jump out of an airplane with the parachute

Doing what you need to do to feel more than alive

Life is about more than survival; it's about thriving

Take a personal trip

Alone

With company

Do something extraordinary that you could never picture the old you doing

This isn't the old you now, is it?

Wisdom

More than just knowledge, it's experience

Past experience and current

It is everything you have learned about as a person

More importantly it is what we learn about ourselves that matters the most

What you enjoy doing

What makes us feel the most vibrant version of ourselves

How we relax

How we communicate

What we need

What we want

How what we want in life can sometimes be the thing we need

Life isn't about hardly making it

It's about how you treat yourself daily

How you let others treat you

Where you want to go

~

What you want to pursue

From the music you like to the thing that helps you get up every day

It could be the sun, the moon, family, yourself

Even a simple count off that NASA does

Five, four, three, two, one, and liftoff

You got this, no matter what anyone else has said, no matter what type of apocalypse is happening today—you completely got this

It is knowing you can handle it and thrive in it that brings you wisdom

Wisdom isn't given but acquired

You can listen to others and know that you want something different

You can observe and know you would never do that

You can experience something and say, "I will never let that happen again"

You can feel it within you, what is right and wrong for you

Once you embrace all of that

You know you have wisdom

～

Acknowledgments

I want to thank my therapist for really helping me find myself. Special shout out to my step mom and my dad for loving and supporting me! I want to thank my friend AJ Sutton for always being there for me! I also want to say thank you to Jada Doeden for being my best friend and supporting me all these years. I am also thankful for Richard Sutton who helped me see that the world can be a brighter place. A special thanks to some teachers! To all of my i-lead teachers, they gave me a place to expand my knowledge and gave me a home away from home. And to every English teacher I had, each and every one of them supported my writing and encouraged me to keep going. I want to thank an old friend of mine named David, he really helped me keep moving forward in life, he told me "There is so much out there you just have to go for it Kenzie." I also want to thank my grandmother for helping me through childhood and getting me here. I also want to thank an old friend who encouraged me to write and actually used to check my old stories when we were younger. Finally I want to thank any of my new found friends, and anyone I missed. I hope you all know that I took in everything you have taught me and now my inner fire burns brighter than before.